Family
Therapy

Elaine Landau

Franklin Watts
A Division of Scholastic Inc.
New York • Toronto • London • Auckland • Sydney
Mexico City • New Delhi • Hong Kong
Danbury, Connecticut

Dedication

For Jerry, Bianca, and Abraham Sanchez

Cover design by Robert O'Brien.
Interior design by Kathleen Santini.

Library of Congress Cataloging-in-Publication Data

Landau, Elaine.
    Family therapy / by Elaine Landau.
        p. cm. — (Life balance)
Summary: Discusses how family therapy works and the types of
conflicts in which it can be helpful.
Includes bibliographical references and index.
    ISBN 0-531-12216-6 (lib. bdg.)   0-531-16611-2 (pbk.)
1. Family psychotherapy—Juvenile literature. 2. Adolescent psychotherapy—Juvenile literature. [1. Family psychotherapy 2.
Counseling] I. Title. II. Series.
    RC488.5.L3488 2004
    616.89'156—dc21
                                    2003007155

Table of Contents

Different Kinds of Families

Fourteen-year-old Jennifer Bradshaw (all names have been changed) used to love Christmas. Ever since she could remember, it had been her favorite holiday. It wasn't just the presents. It was trimming the tree with her mother and brother, planning and preparing Christmas dinner, and, of course, the Bradshaw's traditional Christmas Scrabble game. Everyone in Jennifer's family loved to play Scrabble, and on Christmas after a huge midday meal, the Bradshaws would play their "guys versus girls" game. In Jennifer's family, that meant Jennifer and her mother played against Jennifer's father and brother.

Jennifer used to count the days until Christmas—that is, until two years ago, when her parents got divorced. At that point, her whole life seemed to change. "It wasn't just losing Christmas," she said, "or even the way we celebrated it. It was like losing everything. We stopped doing the things we always did as a family. Now there's never anybody around. I have lots of time to myself. Too much time."

What Jennifer felt is not uncommon in divorce situations. Following her parents' divorce, everyone in her family seemed to go his or her own way. Last year, that felt especially true at Christmas. No one knew what her father's plans for the holiday were. He didn't live near them anymore. A few months after the divorce he'd taken a job across the country, and now Jennifer only saw him when school was out of session in the summer. That year, he'd sent her and her brother their Christmas presents in November and told them to have a great holiday.

Jennifer's brother was also absent at Christmas, because he and three of his college fraternity brothers spent the holiday at a ski lodge. Jennifer thought she'd be spending Christmas with her mother, but that never happened, either. As it turned out, her mother's boyfriend had offered to take her to a fabulous Florida resort for the holiday, a romantic getaway for just the two of them. Jennifer's mother had asked her if she'd mind spending Christmas with their neighbors that year. Jennifer minded a great deal, but felt she couldn't tell her mother that. "I didn't want to wreck Mom's Christmas," she later explained. "I knew that she couldn't afford to go on her own and take me with her. I *had* to say it was okay."

So that was how Jennifer wound up spending Christmas with the Lomes, who lived across the street. It wasn't as bad as she expected. Jennifer could see that the Lomes made a special effort to make her feel welcome. They went out of their way to include her in their conversations and even bought her a Christmas gift. In the end, Jennifer felt glad that she had a nice place to be, but as she watched this loving family interact, she wished that her parents had never divorced.

"When my mom and dad split up, they gave us the usual speech," Jennifer recalled. "You know, the one most kids get when their parents divorce. They said that they would always love me and be there for me. Well, they might be there if I got hit by a truck or something like that. But neither of them was around for Christmas."

Though Jennifer refused to admit it, she felt cheated by her parents' divorce and wanted things to be the way they used to be. Lately, Jennifer felt as if the usual roles in her family had been reversed. Now it felt as if *she* had to be the parent and comfort her mother and father. They wanted to hear that she was doing well and that their divorce hadn't harmed her. But Jennifer *was* affected by their breakup. Though she felt sorry for her parents, she knew that she

"When my mom and dad split up," Jennifer recalled, "they said that they would always love me and be there for me. Well, they might be there if I got hit by a truck or something like that. But neither of them was around for Christmas."

needed more time and affection from them. The problem was that no one but Jennifer seemed to realize that.

Family Structure

A family is like a miniature universe. In many ways, it helps its members meet some of their most basic needs. Often, people tend to think that the family they were born into will never change. But that isn't usually the case. Families are not static. They grow and change over time, just as the people in them do. When Jennifer Bradshaw's family changed, she felt as if she no longer had a family. With her father living thousands of miles away and her brother off at school, it was only Jennifer and her mother at home.

But when family members leave the house, it does not mean they have left the family or they no longer have an impact on how others in the family feel and act. Sometimes, their impact can be even greater when they are not there physically. For example, Jennifer thought about cutting her hair short over Christmas break. Her father had always loved his daughter's beautiful, long dark brown hair. He said that it reminded him of his mother, and when he lived with the family, he would plead with her never to cut it.

Now Jennifer didn't feel much like pleasing her father. She was angry with him for leaving her. Jennifer left the scissors in the drawer, but it was obvious that distance did not make a difference. Even though her father was many states away, he still could affect how she felt greatly.

Before her parents' divorce, Jennifer lived in what might have seemed like the "All-American family." That's the family that's frequently portrayed in advertisements for vacation homes and restaurants. It usually consists of a happily married couple, two kids, and a dog. Yet, according to U.S. census statistics, only 28 percent of Americans have that type of family.

Instead, many different types of families exist in the United States today. The reality of what most modern families look like often differs sharply from the All-American family image. There are single-parent families, stepfamilies, and gay and lesbian families, to name a few.

The "All-American family" usually consists of a happily married couple, two kids, and a dog. Yet, according to U.S. census statistics, only 28 percent of Americans have that type of family.

A Menu of Families

The old saying "two kids and a collie" is no longer true in describing today's family. You can probably find the types of families listed here in your neighborhood.

Married Nuclear Family

This family is the "traditional" family unit we most often think of. There's a husband, a wife, and children. In the traditional married nuclear family, the husband works outside the home, while the wife works at home, taking care of the children and the house.

Statistics show that, over the years, the traditional married nuclear family's form has changed somewhat. The change usually has to do with a shift in work roles within the family unit. In 2 percent of married nuclear families, the husband and wife's traditional roles are now reversed. The wife works outside the home and the husband cares for the children and the house. But there's an even bigger change. More than ever before, both parents in the married nuclear family are employed outside the home. Today, nearly 60 percent of married women with children under six years of age leave the house each morning for work.

Single-Parent Families

In this type of family, there is only one parent. Sometimes, single-parent families result from divorce or the death of a parent. Other times, a person wants children, but prefers not to marry. Eighty-eight percent of all single-parent households are headed by women. It's estimated that more than half of all U.S. children will spend some time in a single-parent household.

Stepfamilies

Stepfamilies, or blended families, as they are sometimes called, are formed when a divorced or widowed person with children remarries. In such families, children who are not biologically related often live in the same home. Stepfamilies are becoming increasingly common. Many young people living in the United States have gone from being part of a married nuclear family to being part of a single-parent household to being part of a stepfamily in just a few years.

Cross-Generational Families

In these situations, adults of different generations within a family live together. Children are often part of cross-generational families. An example of a cross-generational family would be that of a mother who lives with her adult daughter's family. Often, in these families, the grandparents help with finances or childcare. In other cases, a family may care for an elderly grandparent who is ill. In still other situations, children may live with their grandparents if their parents unexpectedly die. All of these are examples of cross-generational families.

A Menu of Families
(Continued)

Joint-Custody Families

Young people living in this type of family are raised by two parents who do not live together. They usually spend part of the
week with one parent and the rest of the week with the other.
In these families, the parents must live fairly close to one another
so that the children can attend the same school every day.

Extended Families

Extended families contain relatives beyond the married nuclear
family that all live under the same roof. Extended families may
include cousins, aunts, or uncles. Often, these family members
work together or share expenses and household tasks.

Cohabitation Families

These are families in which two adults who are not married
or otherwise related live together. Sometimes, they have
children of their own. Other times, children from former
relationships live with them. Most gay and lesbian families
are part of this grouping.

Foster Families

Foster families provide a substitute family for children whose
parents are temporarily unable to care for them.

Healthy Families

A family's structure has nothing to do with how well it functions or meets the needs of its members. Any type of family can be either dysfunctional (unhealthy) or functional (healthy).

People have different ideas about what a healthy family is. Sometimes, these notions are realistic while in other instances, they may be based on the perfection portrayed in television sitcoms. At first, Jennifer Bradshaw thought the only healthy type of family was one in which both parents lived with their children. Yet as time passed, she was able to look past Christmas dinners and family Scrabble games and admit that everything wasn't always rosy at her house. Sometimes, her parents fought bitterly, and there had even been times when her father had hit her mother.

So what makes a family healthy? Researchers have studied families around the globe to see what makes some work well and others fall apart. They came up with nine traits common to healthy families everywhere. The best-functioning families had these traits in common, regardless of race, religion, or income.

- *Caring*—In a healthy family, people care about one another. They show concern when things go wrong and joy when things go well for any family member. They care about each others' feelings and can be counted on for help or advice.

- *Appreciation*—In a well-functioning family, people appreciate each other. Children appreciate the hard work a parent puts into making their favorite meal or the extra hours a parent worked so they can have the school supplies they need. Parents appreciate their children as well. They are grateful that their children try their best in school and can be counted on to do the right thing, even if the parents aren't always there to watch them.

- *Spending time together*—Healthy families spend time together and thrive on shared experiences. Families in which everyone has a busy schedule still find time to do this. Some make a point of having dinner together on most nights. Others plan special family outings or have a designated game or movie night.

- *Encouragement*—In a healthy family, members encourage each other during challenging times. They become one another's "cheerleaders." This usually begins early on. When a baby takes his or her first step, the rest of the family usually bursts into smiles and applause. This continues as the young person does well in school or makes the soccer team. Ideally, young people should be able to count on their family's encouragement to help them reach their full potential.

- *Commitment*—In well-functioning families, members are committed to keeping the family intact. This means that, at times, family members will put their family above their immediate personal pleasure. Family life is a high priority for them.

- *Able to cope with change*—Healthy families are strong and flexible. They adapt well to change and find new, effective ways to handle life's ups and downs. Sometimes, things change when a family member becomes seriously ill or a parent loses a job. There will be new stresses, and the roles within the family may shift, but healthy families get through these rough times. The ability to cope with change is especially evident among the many healthy immigrant families that come to the United States. Often, they don't know the language or are not yet financially secure, but they soon adjust, and their families thrive.

- *Spirituality*—Healthy families tend to believe in a higher power. In religious families, this may be a god. Other families may simply believe in the power of a strong family unit.

- *Community ties*—Well-functioning families do not live in isolation. They are actively involved in their communities through friends, sports, clubs, or religious organizations. They eagerly bring new thoughts and ideas from the outside world into their families to enrich them.

- *Clear roles*—In healthy families, the members have clear-cut roles. They do what is expected of them knowing that this is what's best for them as well as for the rest of the family. However, family roles are flexible and family members have a say about what their roles are within the families.

Troubled Families

In an ideal world, all families would function well. Divorce, infidelity, substance abuse, child molestation, power struggles, incest, poor communication, sibling rivalry, and a host of other problems would never occur.

Unfortunately, that is not the case. Today, more than 50 percent of all marriages end in divorce. A family split can be painful for both the adults and the children involved. It certainly was for Jennifer Bradshaw. Nevertheless, family problems do not always stem from divorce. Even families that remain intact can face serious issues.

At times, everyone in a family may dream of a harmonious family life, but the family members can't seem to stop fighting. Some continue fighting for years. Many of these people feel both anger and shame about their family lives. The situation may not look that bad to outsiders, but inwardly, family members often feel as if they are slowly drowning in negativity. In other families, problems quickly escalate into highly charged, emotional battles. They find themselves faced with one crisis after another.

Yet families in conflict do not always stay that way. Some families have gotten help and turned things around. People often improve individually by attending counseling sessions or by taking medication if there's a biological reason for their personality problems. Individual counseling focuses on an individual's behavior and how that person sees the world. Troubled families, however, take a different route. They need a method that treats the whole family. This process is known as family therapy.

A New Form of Treatment

Family therapy is a fairly new form of treatment. It came into being in the 1950s after a group of doctors treating patients with schizophrenia noticed that their patients were greatly affected by what went on in their families. Schizophrenia is a serious mental illness in which a person can suffer from a variety of serious symptoms. While schizophrenics generally function best when treated with prescription medications, the doctors realized that medication simply wasn't enough.

They found that their schizophrenic patients' conditions became worse when their families argued and improved when things went well with family members. These doctors came to see the family as an important influence that could not be ignored. They recognized that each family has its own rules and ways of doing things, as well as methods of communication. As a result, the doctors began treating the families of their schizophrenic patients along with the patients in their therapy sessions.

Since that time, the family has been recognized as an extremely important factor in people's lives. It not only affects people with serious illnesses, such as schizophrenia, but can have a significant bearing on people's success at school and work as well as on their relationships with others. Just as an unhealthy person can improve with proper treatment, it's been found that the same is true for an unhealthy family. The result has been the development and growth of family therapy.

The family can have a significant bearing on people's success at school and work as well as on their relationships with others.

Today, family therapy is a recognized and highly regarded form of treatment. Marriage and family therapists (MFTs) are trained professionals who have either a master's or doctoral degree in marriage and family therapy, along with at least two years of experience working with patients. In most areas, marriage and family therapists are licensed by the state in which they practice. According to the American Association for Marriage and Family Therapy, MFTs are concerned with the "overall long-term well-being of individuals and their families

… addressing a wide array of relationship issues within the context of the family system."

MFTs are mental health professionals. Mental health has been defined as a person's psychological state. Good mental health is reflected in all aspects of a person's life—social, spiritual, and economic. MFTs help clients achieve and maintain good mental health within the family unit.

People have turned to family therapy to fix problems, repair relationships, or take their family's functioning to a higher level. Jennifer, along with her mother and brother, eventually sought family therapy. After a time, they realized that they were still a family even though Mr. Bradshaw was gone. They went to family therapy to see how they could become a stronger family and give each other the encouragement and support they needed. MFTs have improved life for families throughout the United States. At any given time, they are treating more than 1.8 million people.

Family Therapy
Two
in Action

Question: In which of the following cases do you think family therapy might be useful?

Case #1: Jason's parents have barely spoken to each other since their divorce. When they have to talk to one another, they usually scream. They have also turned Jason and his younger sister Beth into unwilling messengers, forced to carry emotionally charged messages from one parent to another. Often, their parents get so angry about the messages that they end up screaming at the children. As a result, everyone feels miserable.

Case #2: Shari and Alana Rosen's grandmother lived with their family until she died last year. During her illness, Shari and Alana had helped their mother care for the ailing woman. The teenage girls had always been extremely attached to their grandmother, but caring for her took up a good deal of their time. For almost a year, they gave up nearly all their after-school activities and many of their weekends. Their grandmother died on the night of Shari's junior prom. Although the girls had known that their grandmother had little time left to live, they had a hard time adjusting to her death.

Case #3: Twelve-year-old Kevin set fire to his junior high school during Christmas vacation. No one was in the building at the time, so luckily, no one was hurt. Kevin claimed he did it because he was afraid of failing math. He hoped that the fire would destroy any evidence of his poor test scores. Though Kevin denies it, the authorities suspect that this wasn't the first fire he's set.

Did you pick case 1, 2, or 3 as a good candidate for family therapy? Regardless of the one you chose, you're right. Family therapy would be useful in all of these cases. This form of treatment is frequently used to handle a broad range of problems. According to the Kentucky Association for Marriage and Family, family therapy is often helpful with the following concerns:

- Persistent problems with a child's behavior, school adjustment, or performance

- Feelings of depression, failure, anxiety, or loneliness
- Difficulty in communicating (sharing ideas and feelings) with family members, friends, or coworkers
- Alcohol or drug abuse
- Ongoing financial difficulties
- Drastic weight fluctuations or irregular eating patterns
- Chronic work difficulties or frequent job changes
- Unmanageable anger or hostility
- Persistent feelings of dissatisfaction with marriage or family life
- Difficulty coping with stresses arising from a life crisis, such as death, divorce, acute or chronic illness, or unemployment

The Idea Behind Family Therapy

Family therapy is based on the notion that the problem at hand lies within the family network rather than in any one individual. In this type of therapy, the family unit is looked at as a whole. It is seen as a complete system in which the various relationships between all family members have a bearing on the problem. Because the family is viewed as a system, this form of treatment is sometimes called systemic family therapy.

You might wonder how family therapy could possibly work for Kevin, the twelve-year-old who set his school on

Family therapy is based on the notion that the problem at hand lies within the family network rather than in any one individual.

fire. Many people would readily think that, in this instance, the problem rests with the boy. Yet, a closer examination of the case reveals that Kevin, as well as his family, could greatly benefit from family therapy.

As it turned out, Kevin had an extremely troubled home life. His father had a serious drinking problem and was unable to hold down a job. Kevin's mother had recently given birth to a baby girl. It was a difficult birth, and there had been complications. She had to spend several weeks in bed afterward. Kevin's aunt had stayed with the family for a while to help, but she was too busy caring for the baby and Kevin's mother to pay very much attention to Kevin.

Kevin felt a great deal of anger and resentment toward his father. He had spent too many hours hiding in the closet during his father's drunken binges to feel that he could ever respect him. He was upset about his father's inability to provide for his family and felt ashamed that they rarely had the money for the things he needed or wanted.

Kevin believed that his mother had let him down as well. She often seemed too overwhelmed by the family's problems to be much help to him. Kevin blamed her for marrying his father and then not having the courage to stand up to him. He already sensed that the new baby was only going to be one more headache in their already chaotic life.

Despite his young age, after the fire, Kevin was in serious trouble with the law. He was ordered by the juvenile court to go to individual therapy. Unlike family therapy, in individual therapy, the emphasis is placed on the patient or client (the individual in treatment). That person works on a one-to-one basis with a professional therapist to gain insight into his or her thoughts and feelings. The person gains a deeper understanding of why he or she sometimes feels compelled to act in a certain way. This understanding serves as a first step in helping that individual change for the better. Some therapists also feel it is important to delve into a client's past. This is done to see how past experiences may have a bearing on the person's present problems.

While individual therapy was helpful for Kevin, his therapist recommended that he also be in family therapy. She felt that Kevin would have a hard time making personal changes unless things changed in his home life as well. Kevin and the other members of his family needed to learn better ways to communicate and relate to one another. They would also have to learn how to make better choices in various areas of their lives. These are goals that can be accomplished through family therapy.

Family Therapy at Work

All family members attend family therapy sessions. In some cases, even members of the extended family, such as grandparents, become part of the process. This may depend on whether members of the extended family live with the family or how much of an influence they have on what happens within the family unit.

Here, the expression "No man is an island" comes into play. Family therapists stress that family relationships affect everyone in the family unit. At first, it may not seem obvious, but how people interact with other family members often affects their feelings and actions. A good example of this can be seen in Jason's story, case #1.

Jason's parents handled their divorce like a prizefight in which both former spouses were determined to score a knockout. Unfortunately, their actions took a serious toll on their children. Using Jason and his younger sister Beth as messengers put the children in an extremely difficult position. They hated being in the middle of things and wished that their parents would leave them out of their arguments.

After several months of living in what felt like a pressure cooker, Jason's grades began to drop. It wasn't long before he started cutting classes. When his school counselor spoke to him, Jason said it was hard being at school and even harder being at home, and sometimes he felt like he "just had to cut loose." Jason's younger sister Beth was showing signs of stress too. She began wetting her bed at night, something she hadn't done in years.

Jason's family sought family therapy. In their case, there was a dramatic improvement soon afterward. With the therapist's help, Jason's parents learned to stop using their children destructively. It was agreed that Jason and Beth would not deliver messages from their parents any longer, and that their parents would try to keep things calm around them. Within a few weeks, Jason's sister's bed-wetting stopped and Jason was regularly attending classes again. Both children said that it was easier for them to accept their parents' divorce after attending family therapy.

The approach taken in Jason and Beth's case is typical of the way problems are seen in family therapy. Family therapy focuses on making changes within the family as a whole. Beth's bed-wetting and Jason's cutting classes were not viewed as the children's personal problems, but as symptoms of an ailing family that was negatively affecting its members.

In family therapy, all the family members help identify

problems that might be a source of trouble. Everyone is encouraged to come up with ways to solve these difficulties. Both parents and children are asked to express their feelings and voice their opinions. Jason, as well as his little sister, had an opportunity to let their parents know how uncomfortable they felt when caught in the middle of their arguments. For the first time, they also let them know how sad they were that the whole family was no longer living together. This helped their parents see more clearly the effects of their actions on their children. While they were not prepared to reunite, they were ready to make some important changes in the way they treated the children. In family therapy sessions, everyone counts.

The Role of the Family Therapist

Family therapists have an important role in the process. They help the family members to change and grow. To do this, they must first evaluate the family. Sometimes they'll ask probing questions to draw information out of family members. They may ask what brought the family into treatment and see how the various family members answer (or do not answer) this question. They can glean a lot of information by seeing who agrees with whom, who is quick to assign blame, and who is willing to accept being thought of as the culprit in question.

One Family, Two Therapists

While family therapy can be done with just one therapist, at times, two therapists team up to work with a family. This is especially helpful in families in which the husband and wife are continuously fighting. In these situations, a male and female therapist usually work together. The positive way the two treat each other serves as an important example to the parents. Husbands and wives can model their behavior after the therapists' behavior and improve the way they relate to one another. Children in treatment also see what things can be like when adults deal sensibly and calmly with emotionally charged issues.

In other cases, a therapist may quietly observe the family interacting for a while. It usually isn't long before the therapist becomes familiar with the different roles people play within the family structure. Who really runs things? Does someone continually assume the role of the victim? Is there a family "bad boy"? How do the various family members

Family therapists can glean a lot of information by seeing who agrees with whom, who is quick to assign blame, and who is willing to accept being thought of as the culprit in question.

communicate with each other? These are all important questions that will be explored during these sessions.

The therapist must also see if subsystems exist within the family. Subsystems are smaller groups that form within the family. Do some family members tend to side with certain others? What do they gain by doing so? It is important for the therapist to know if emotional triangles have developed within the family as well. Emotional triangles form when two family members have a difficult time

An Explosive Emotional Triangle

Some emotional triangles can be counted on to cause fireworks. A common triangle often occurs between a wife, a husband, and the husband's mother. When this triangle develops, the wife may see her mother-in-law as an unwelcome intruder who inappropriately controls her adult son. The mother-in-law, on the other hand, is usually equally disenchanted with her son's wife. To her, the younger woman may seem like a thief who has stolen her son's heart and is determined to shut her out of the couple's life. While neither of their perceptions may be accurate, the women involved feel as if they are. Meanwhile, though the husband may appear to be upset over what's happening, on some level, he may enjoy being fought over by the two most important women in his life.

dealing with one another. To smooth things over, a third family member is drawn into the equation. The third person acts as a buffer between the two, helping to stabilize their relationship. Perhaps the most common family triangle is formed when a feuding husband and wife use a child in that manner.

The therapist is on everyone's side because his or her "patient" is the entire family.

Throughout the treatment sessions, family therapists remain neutral. They leave their personal feelings at the door and do not side with one family member over another. The therapist is on everyone's side because his or her "patient" is the entire family. The therapist is there to help enhance the family as a working system.

During the first few sessions, the family therapist creates an atmosphere in which all family members feel free to speak. It is especially important that family members believe that they are in a safe, caring setting. They must feel comfortable enough to admit embarrassing feelings or actions.

This became a factor with Shari and Alana Rosen, case #2. While Shari and Alana loved their grandmother and were glad to have helped with her care, there were times when both girls would rather have been with their friends.

Too ashamed to voice these feelings while their grand-mother was alive, both experienced feelings of guilt after her death. Neither girl felt entitled to resume her life as a carefree teen. "Sometimes I wished that Grandma had gone into a nursing home," Shari said. "I hated myself for it. She was so good to me when I was little. I used to go to her house on weekends and she'd bake cookies for me. If she gave up her weekends to take care of me, how could I mind giving up mine for her when she was so sick? I didn't want to feel the way I did. I tried not to, but I couldn't help it."

In family therapy, both Shari and Alana were finally able to admit the feelings they'd held in. The therapist helped them realize that what they'd experienced was normal. They also had a chance to discuss the positives they'd gained from having their grandmother live with them through her illness. The girls' mother benefited from the sessions too. She finally allowed herself to grieve openly for her loss. Before going to family therapy, she always felt that she had to keep smiling for her daughters' sake. Family therapy helped the Rosens get on with their lives.

Setting Goals

Together, the therapist and the family define specific goals that will help improve family life for everyone. The most pressing problems or those that have been most disruptive to the family are tackled first. People in family therapy do not undergo personality makeovers. After some realistic goals are set, however, it is up to each family member to do whatever is necessary to help achieve them.

Both adults and young people can learn a lot during family therapy sessions. Usually, everyone discovers better ways of letting his or her feelings be known. Once a feeling of openness has been created, it's easier for them to be honest about problems. Through family therapy, all family members see how they can better relate to one another.

Characteristics of Family Therapy

Many people praise family therapy for helping them achieve positive change in a short amount of time. Individual therapy can go on for years as a client and therapist work on long-term goals, such as personality change. But family therapy offers a different sort of treatment program. The American Association for Marriage and Family Therapy describes family therapy as being all of the following:

- *Brief*—Family therapy is what is known as short-term therapy. A short-term treatment program usually consists of about twelve to fifteen sessions. Family therapy is designed to get to the heart of a problem relatively quickly. This is important for offering the family relief quickly. It also helps keep the cost of treatment low. Many people cannot afford years of expensive individual treatment and, for some, family therapy provides an economical alternative.

- *Solution focused*—Part of the family therapist's task is to identify possible solutions and steer the family in that direction during their time together. Family therapy is geared toward providing answers to a family's problems.

- *Having specific, reasonable goals*—In family therapy, the therapist helps the family to separate achievable goals from unrealistic dreams. The therapist also assists clients in breaking down these goals into manageable units so they can be more readily achieved. Families may also design their own reward system as an incentive for all members to work toward the defined goals.

- *Designed with an end in mind*—The family therapist keeps the family on track during their time together. The therapist will also introduce ways to handle similar difficulties that could arise in the future.

Though families may attend therapy for numerous reasons, many seek it out because of specific problems

Paying for Family Therapy

Today, many health insurance plans cover the cost of family therapy. Not every plan does, however, and not everyone has health insurance. In response, the American Association for Marriage and Family Therapy reports that family therapists are now offering "consumer-friendly" services that are more affordable and accessible to their clients. These include having evening and weekend hours so their clients don't have to lose money by taking time off from work to attend appointments. Many have also introduced sliding fee scales, where clients are charged therapy fees in keeping with their incomes. Some family therapists also offer new therapy services such as lower cost, brief (15-minute) check-up visits to see that the family remains on course.

with teenagers, stepfamilies, and dealing with illness and loss. Family therapy can help in these situations, as will be discussed in the chapters ahead.

Three

The Teen Challenge

"We don't have any problems at home. It's just that our daughter has been getting into so much trouble lately," Mrs. Pike told the family therapist. Though the Pikes never thought they'd be going to see a family therapist, fifteen-year-old Lynn Pike had not been doing well in school, and recently, things had gotten worse.

Lynn was also having trouble with her part-time job at the public library. After getting into a heated argument with the head librarian, she stormed out of the building and never went back. Lynn had always loved the library and the people who worked there. Now Lynn refused to go to the library at all, even to do homework. Of course, that didn't help her plummeting grades.

In the last few months, Lynn had been getting into arguments with just about everyone. She stopped seeing two friends she had been close with since third grade, and she had lots of battles at home. Lynn had already been sent to see the school counselor. After speaking with Lynn's parents, the counselor suggested that Lynn start seeing a private therapist for individual counseling sessions. The therapist met with Lynn and her parents and felt that the Pike family would benefit from attending family therapy.

The Hidden Problem

Lynn's parents thought their daughter's poor behavior was the only problem. However, the therapist showed them that there was actually another way to look at the situation. First, she urged the Pikes to stop finger-pointing, assuring them that simply placing the blame on Lynn was not going to improve matters. Instead, their therapy centered on getting to the heart of the problem. One vital question needed to be asked: Was something happening within the family that could have contributed to Lynn's change in behavior? As it turned out, the reasons for Lynn's actions were not as mysterious as they had seemed. In part, Lynn was reacting to her parents' continual arguments about money.

The Pikes had no idea that their daughter was aware of their financial disputes, even though these conflicts were part of their everyday lives. Mr. Pike felt that his wife used credit cards too freely, making it impossible for the family to get ahead or even to make ends meet. Mrs. Pike, on the other hand, saw her husband as stingy and never hesitated to say so. She would frequently chide him for what she viewed as his not caring whether his family "had the finer things in life."

While snide remarks about money were made as offhandedly as comments about the weather, neither Mr. nor Mrs. Pike viewed this as a problem. Both of Lynn's parents were careful to say what was really on their minds only after Lynn went to bed. However, Lynn heard and understood every word of what was said. She was also keenly aware of how harshly her parents treated one another.

Lynn hated the continual bickering, which she described as going on in her house twenty-four hours a day, seven days a week. While she often heard her mother tell people what a great marriage she had, Lynn never quite believed it. She felt as if there was always an unspoken fight going on, and she didn't want to have to take sides. However, Lynn's parents made it hard not to. Whenever her father drove Lynn to her job at the library, he always praised her for working. At the same time, he would put her mother down, saying that even though his wife had a college degree, she was "too busy" to get a job and help out the family financially. Lynn liked her job at the library, but felt guilty for working because she didn't want to make her mother look bad.

Lynn also felt pressured by her mother to side with her. When the two went shopping together, her mother always called her father cheap. If Lynn refused to agree, her mother would clam up and barely speak to her for the rest of the day. When she and her mother bought new clothes or cosmetics, Mrs. Pike insisted that Lynn lie about their purchases, hiding all the boxes from her father. Mrs. Pike wanted to avoid an argument with her husband until the credit card bill arrived. However, Lynn's father knew his wife too well to be fooled. After Mrs. Pike left the room, he would pressure his daughter to tell him the truth.

Lynn had kept up this balancing act between her parents for years. She wasn't even aware that she was doing it. It was part of her life, but it seemed to be taking up an increasing amount of her emotional energy. Things nearly reached a breaking point when Lynn overheard her parents having an especially vicious argument one night, when her father threatened to leave for good if her mother didn't stop her wasteful spending. The thought made Lynn sick to her stomach. Her father had left once before when Lynn was much younger, but he was only gone for a few weeks. Lynn strongly suspected that her father had given the marriage another try for her sake. Now she felt that it was up to her to hold her parents' marriage together again.

Lynn strongly suspected that her father had given the marriage another try for her sake. Now she felt that it was up to her to hold her parents' marriage together again.

Letting In the Light

While Lynn had not been able to tell her parents how she felt, she opened up in family therapy. After several sessions, Lynn realized that she had started an argument with the librarian at work to have an excuse to quit her job. She hadn't wanted to leave; she just wanted to stop feeling guilty about making her mother look bad.

The therapist worked with Lynn's parents as well. Neither had been consciously aware of the effect their financial disputes had on Lynn. The couple had been squabbling over money for so long that arguing about it had simply become part of their lives. Yet these often-biting exchanges were destructive to their daughter and their family as a whole.

After a number of family therapy sessions, Mr. and Mrs. Pike were sent to a marriage counselor for further treatment. They agreed not to put Lynn in the middle of any more arguments. The family would also try to find some moderately priced activities they could all enjoy together. Things began to improve within a few months. Lynn felt that a tremendous burden had been lifted from her shoulders. She started doing better in school and began seeing her two best friends again. Although Mr. and Mrs. Pike's differences about money were not immediately resolved, much of the anger and tension in the family had been diffused.

Marriage Counseling

In some ways, marriage therapy is similar to family therapy, except the therapist works only with a couple. This is important because husbands and wives who don't get along often produce families that don't get along. During the sessions, the therapist helps the couple identify strengths within the marriage and build on those. The couple also usually develops better ways to relate to one another. This can include learning techniques that allow a husband and wife to make their feelings known without attacking the partner. Couples can also develop better listening skills so that each is better able to hear what his or her partner is trying to say.

The Family Photo Exercise

To gain more insight into the Pike's difficulties, their therapist used a family therapy technique known as family photos.

Lynn and her parents were asked to go through their family photo albums at home and bring in one photograph that was special to them. They were told to be prepared to discuss why they had chosen it.

The purpose of this exercise is to give both the therapist and the family members more insight into the family's relationships and roles. As the therapist had hoped, the various photographs the Pikes brought in proved to be quite revealing. Mrs. Pike picked one of the family members before they left for church on Easter Sunday. They were all dressed up in their Sunday best, and Mrs. Pike looked like she had just stepped out of a fashion magazine.

It was clear from the picture that Lynn's mother cared a great deal about appearances. She admitted that perhaps she always wanted to look good because she did not feel confident about herself. She confided that part of this came from feeling that she hadn't been the best mother to Lynn. Though her mother didn't know it, Lynn didn't feel that way at all. After Lynn assured her mother that she'd done many wonderful things for her over the years, Mrs. Pike felt better about herself. Apparently, that was something she had always wanted to hear.

Interestingly, Mr. Pike and Lynn picked the same photograph to bring to therapy. It was one of the family hiking on a beautiful autumn day. They were on a nature trail not far from their home. The Pikes hadn't gone hiking in years, but that was one of the activities all the Pikes agreed that they wanted to do again.

Though the Pike's therapist had them bring in one photograph each, some family therapists do the photo exercise differently. They ask the family to bring their whole photo album to therapy sessions. The therapist and family members look at the pictures together. At times, family therapists find that going through photos of the family's past can help bring feelings to life that have long been buried.

Teen Problems Improved

Many families that have ended up in family therapy because of a teenager's behavior problems have had good experiences. According to the American Association for Marriage and Family Therapy, nearly 90 percent of family therapy clients report an improvement in their attitudes following treatment. Young people who have undergone family therapy frequently show an improvement in school performance, and children and teens seem to have fewer conflicts with their classmates and friends. In almost 74 percent of cases, parents report a noticeable improvement in the young person's overall behavior as well.

Family therapy's success with teens may be due partly to the nature of the process. It's a type of therapy in which everyone's voice is heard, and all family members' feelings are considered. Unfortunately, young people are not always given this courtesy in our society. That could also be why this method has been shown to be successful with young people living in stepfamilies, the topic of the next chapter. There, two separate families face the challenge of combining effectively. Often, family therapy can help families get over the bumps in the road.

Four

The Stepfamily
Challenge

"It's not fair," says Joel, age seventeen. "They cheated me. Gypped by my own parents. We were supposed to be a family. My parents go and divorce and my father marries this crazy woman. She moves in with her four miserable brats. It's like invading aliens. We don't have room for them— our house is small enough as it is. People can report bad businesses to the Better Business Bureau, but where do you go when your parents cheat you? There is no Better Parents Bureau. There ought to be."

It's not hard to see that Joel feels cheated. This situation created many important changes in his life that he had not chosen for himself. Worse yet, he felt as if he had lost control over nearly everything that mattered to him.

"No One Asked Me"

Joel's parents divorced when he was just three years old. His mother did not feel able to care for a child on her own, so Joel lived with his father. In the past, his father had often dated. Joel was used to meeting different women through the years. They would come to his Little League games and sometimes even to the science fairs at his school.

He liked some of them a little, but the best thing about his father's relationships was that they never lasted. Living alone with his dad suited Joel just fine. Now nothing was the same. Nina and her four children were there to stay.

Overnight, Joel went from being an only child to being the oldest of five. He didn't like being the "big brother," but since his father's wedding, he'd been thrust into that role. At times, that entailed driving his stepsisters to ballet classes, helping them with homework, and running errands for Nina.

No one had ever asked Joel if he wanted to be a part of this new family. He was simply expected to fit in and help out. It was also clear that his father and Nina expected him not to mind that his home had been invaded or that there was a lot less of his father's time available to him. Joel was supposed to love Nina and her children instantly. People called them a blended family, and to the world, they were supposed to be a real-life version of the Brady Bunch.

Joel's negative feelings about being part of a stepfamily are not unusual. In recent years, stepfamilies have become increasingly common. Nearly 80 percent of divorced or widowed people remarry within five years, and in many cases, they have children. It's estimated that in the United States alone, more than 1,300 new stepfamilies are formed every day. Some experts predict that within the twenty-first century, the most common family type will be those with a mixture of children from different marriages.

Some experts predict that within the twenty-first century, the most common family type will be those with a mixture of children from different marriages.

Some people would like to think that stepfamilies and biologically related families are the same. At first glance, they may look alike—there are parents, kids, and often pets. Yet there are some very real differences between the two.

While biologically related families, or biofamilies, live in a single home, this is not always true for stepfamilies. Frequently, children in these situations live with one parent most of the time, but spend weekends, some holidays, or part of the summer with the other. In some joint-custody arrangements, the young person's week is evenly divided between the two homes.

That can be a difficult adjustment for anyone. The transition from having his or her own room in one house to sharing a room with several stepbrothers or stepsisters in the other can lead to conflicts over space, possessions, and privacy. Rules can also differ sharply from one household to another. Dinner hours, homework schedules, and time allowed on the phone or watching television are rarely the same in both places.

That was a big problem for eleven-year-old Jena. At her mother's house, she was allowed to watch as much television as she wanted after finishing her homework. Things were quite different at her father's house. Jena's stepmother felt there were better things to do than watch television, and she and her two stepsisters were not permitted to turn on the television set during the week. There was also a two-hour television limit on weekends.

At times, getting along with everyone in any family can be difficult. However, in stepfamilies, there are many more people to form relationships with. Sometimes young people end up with two sets of parents, a number of stepbrothers and stepsisters, and any half siblings, or new children that result from their parents' remarriages. There may also be many new aunts, uncles, cousins, and grandparents.

Surprisingly, it was his new stepgrandparents who caused difficulties for twelve-year-old Derrick. As Derrick had no grandparents of his own, he was pleased when his stepfather's parents took an interest in him. Whenever they took his stepbrother on outings, they always invited Derrick along. That year, Derrick was glad that his stepgrandparents were spending Christmas with them. At least he was until the gifts were opened. His stepgrandparents had bought Derrick a CD by one of his favorite groups. Derrick was delighted with his gift—it showed that they had taken the time to learn what music he liked and had gone through the trouble of getting the CD for him. He was soon disappointed, however. When his stepbrother opened his gift from them, Derrick saw that he had received a laptop computer. Derrick thought that the difference in their gifts spoke volumes. He felt more like an outsider than ever.

Family Sculpting

Things improved after Derrick's entire family, including his stepgrandparents, began going to family therapy. One family therapy technique that proved especially useful was family sculpting.

Family sculpting is a dynamic way of letting family members know immediately exactly how others in the family perceive what is happening between them. During this exercise, family members take turns placing the people in their family in actual positions they believe best reflects what's going on at home.

Sometimes, a child will have a parent stand on a chair while he or she lies on the floor. This shows that the child sees the parent as extremely powerful, while the child feels lowly and without much power. People seen as very stubborn might be placed with their hands on their hips. A teen who feels isolated, or excluded, from other family members might have them all sitting in a circle as he or she stands alone in the corner.

Derrick's family sculpture was very moving. In it, he had his stepgrandparents embrace his stepbrother while he stood off to the side. Through this family therapy technique, Derrick was able to let his stepgrandparents know what he'd been too uncomfortable to tell them—that he wanted to be closer to them. The couple immediately realized that while they thought they were including Derrick, he was ready for more. He wanted to belong to them the same way his stepbrother did.

Derrick's stepgrandparents were touched by his family sculpture plea. They had always wanted another grandchild, but in some ways had deliberately held back their affection from Derrick, not wanting to overwhelm him. That family therapy session brought about an important change in

Derrick's family. In the months ahead, his stepgrandparents came to love him as their own, and he returned the feelings.

Rules, Routines, and Rituals

Family therapy can be extremely effective in helping stepfamilies bring some order to their lives. This is often done by drawing up house rules. The rules are not automatically set by the parents. Everyone has a say in determining what is fair and what he or she thinks will work. The therapist will stress that the best plan is one that is acceptable to all family members. People are always more willing to follow rules they helped create.

Once the rules are set up, there are usually other compromises to work out. Stepfamilies must deal with situations in which differing lifestyles and expectations can cause problems. In some stepfamilies, one parent may feel that having dinner together is an important family ritual. The other parent, however, may feel more comfortable allowing his or her children to grab a bite at a fast food restaurant before rushing off to a school band rehearsal or a sporting event. While differing routines could lead to misunderstandings and hurt feelings, these situations can be worked through with some preplanning.

Family therapists also help family members see that there is no right or wrong way to celebrate holidays and

Breaking Down the Myths

There are many commonly held myths about stepfamilies. Sometimes people become part of a stepfamily believing that all these things are true. Family therapy helps by offering stepfamilies a realistic view of things. It's a first step, but a very important one.

Many people want their newly formed stepfamily to be perfect, but unfair expectations can put a great deal of pressure on family members. A family therapist can help families develop a view of what to expect that is more on target with reality.

Myth #1: All stepmothers are wicked.
Remember Cinderella's wicked stepmother? Or how about Hansel and Gretel's stepmother, who convinced their father to send his children into the woods alone to die? Snow White's wicked stepmother tried to kill her twice. When a woodsman could not go through with it, she brought out a poison apple.

In family therapy, stereotypes about stepmothers are broken down. Young people begin to see their stepmothers as real people. Like other people, stepmothers feel a broad range of emotions. During the sessions, children and their stepmothers may explore some of the things they actually have in common. The family therapist will help them identify what is good in their relationships. As time passes, the young people and their stepmothers will build on these positives together.

Myth #2: Adjustment to stepfamily life occurs quickly.
Some people think families blend as easily as Smoothies. In fact, nothing could be farther from the truth. In these situations, the family therapist can add a dash of reality to the situation. The therapist can make certain that everyone understands how complex stepfamilies are. Different families have different ways of relating, as well as separate past histories. Through family therapy, family members learn that it takes years for a stepfamily to develop a distinct history of its own.

Myth #3: Children adjust to divorce and remarriage more easily if the biological father (or mother) withdraws.
Don't believe it. Out of sight does not necessarily mean out of mind. Most family therapists don't feel it is wise to cut children off from a biological parent. It does not speed up their adjustment to living in a stepfamily and often makes them feel abandoned by someone important to them. Many therapists try to involve both sets of parents in sessions if the adults are able to work together for the good of the children. The only time a parent should not be involved with his or her child is if the parent abuses or neglects the young person.

Breaking Down the Myths
(Continued)

Myth #4: Stepfamilies that are formed after a parent dies are easier to adapt to.

This is not necessarily true. Usually, children need time to grieve for the lost parent. In some cases, a deceased parent may develop a halo effect. When this happens, the biological parent is remembered as being a saint. In the child's mind, he or she becomes someone who never did any wrong. Even the best stepparent could never measure up to the biological parent's memory. Therefore, comparisons often become unfair and hurtful.

A family therapist can help grieving children go through the necessary stages of mourning. People need to do this to deal with their loss. Family therapists also guide other family members in helping the young people through this process. In addition, a family therapist can help children with any loyalty issues that may arise afterward. In time, the children hopefully come to see that by caring for a new stepparent, they are not betraying a parent who has passed away.

Myth #5: Part-time stepfamilies are easier for children to adapt to.

Families in which stepchildren live far away are not always

better off. Often, these family members do not have enough time together to work through their differences. That makes it hard for them to build a solid family base. As a result, the awkwardness and adjustment period common to new stepfamilies tends to last for a long time.

At times, these part-time arrangements are especially hard on the children. Stepchildren who visit infrequently sometimes feel threatened by children who live full time with their biological mother or father. A family therapist can help them see that their stepbrothers and stepsisters are not stealing their parent's love.

In these situations, the family therapist may find it helpful to introduce a concept that is sometimes referred to as the Apple Pie Theory of Love. According to this theory, there is a limited amount of love in a family to go around. Love, like pie, has to be divided up among those at the family table. Everyone wants the biggest piece and feels jealous of anyone who he or she thinks has a bigger slice. In family therapy, people see that this theory does not apply in real life. The therapist helps the family members see that people are capable of giving unlimited love. Both parents and children can care for many family members without loving any one person less. In healthy, well-functioning families, there is always more than enough love to go around.

other special occasions. In the Bishop family, Mr. Bishop and his children had always prepared a ham for Christmas dinner, but his new wife and her children always had turkey. Because Mrs. Bishop did the cooking, she made a turkey for their first Christmas together. The meal was delicious, but it just didn't feel like Christmas dinner for half of the family. Hoping to please everyone, the following year Mrs. Bishop made both a ham and a turkey for Christmas dinner. That was better, but it made them feel as if two separate families were eating at the dinner table.

Their family therapist suggested that the Bishops come up with their own new traditions. After all, they were a new family. That was precisely what they did for their third Christmas together.

The Bishops may have had different tastes, but everyone in the family loved Chinese food. Therefore, a few months before Christmas, they bought a wok and a Chinese cookbook. Everyone went through the book picking out recipes that looked good. In the weeks before the holiday, they tried out the recipes. Sometimes, they prepared the dishes together. The whole family planned the Christmas dinner menu as well. From appetizers to desserts, only Chinese food would be chosen. The big day went even better than expected, and the family has had Chinese food for Christmas dinner every year since then.

Their family therapist suggested that the Bishops come up with their own new traditions. The family has had Chinese food for Christmas dinner every year since then.

Family therapists feel that all stepfamilies can benefit from creating new traditions that are uniquely their own. These make for positive memories and reduce the tendency for family members to compare holidays with those of the past. Stepfamily members need to be flexible and open to new ideas and ways of trying things. Just like the old saying, "Rome wasn't built in a day," family therapists note that it can take years for stepfamilies to learn to run smoothly. However, time, openness, and hard work can do wonders in these situations.

Five

Illness and **Loss**

Until two years ago, eleven-year-old Ellie Cole thought that she and her nine-year-old sister Sarah were among the luckiest kids in the world. Ellie felt that they had great parents and friends and went to a wonderful school. Their father was a successful electrical engineer, and while their mother had been an elementary school art teacher, she became a stay-at-home mom after the girls were born.

But everything changed two years ago, after Mrs. Cole found a lump in her breast. Though she told her husband, Mrs. Cole kept the news from the girls. She knew it could be breast cancer—her mother had died of it—but she didn't want to make the children panic.

Yet at that point, Ellie knew that something was wrong, and so did Sarah. Their parents hadn't said anything, but they both seemed tense and nervous. "I knew something was up," Ellie later said. "I just didn't know what. Dad said that Mom had to go into the hospital for a few tests. He said that there was nothing to worry about, but I knew he was lying. People don't go into the hospital for nothing, and the last time Mom looked this worried was when Grandma was sick."

The news from the hospital was frightening, but not terribly surprising: Mrs. Cole had breast cancer. Within days, Mrs. Cole underwent surgery, and after that began chemotherapy treatments at the hospital. Ellie wanted to talk to her mother about what was happening, but Mrs. Cole couldn't bring herself to do that yet. She was still too afraid of dying to assure her daughters that she would live.

"I remember that my Dad told us that Mom had breast cancer," Ellie recalled. "I kept thinking about how Grandma died of breast cancer just a few years ago. Now Mom would probably die too. That was all I could think about. It was even hard to sleep at night. Sarah was upset too. I saw that she couldn't study—she couldn't concentrate."

Ellie thought she would feel better when her mother came home from the hospital. A housekeeper was hired to clean the house, do the laundry, cook the meals, and care for Mrs. Cole. Ellie's father said that the housekeeper would keep things running smoothly, but Ellie knew that no one could do that. All Ellie saw was that the housekeeper kept her and Sarah away from their mother, saying that Mrs. Cole needed to save her strength to fight the disease. She wanted her to rest as much as possible. She also did not want the girls to see their mother in such a state, thinking it would upset them. Yet Ellie felt that not seeing her mother at all was upsetting her and Sarah more than seeing her mother ill.

Things began to fall apart at the Cole house. It was no longer the happy place it had once been. Not knowing what to do, Mr. Cole took Ellie's teacher's advice. He sought the help of a family therapist.

Trying Treatment

As it turned out, that was exactly what was needed. The therapist helped everyone in the family deal with the situation better. The doctor felt that Mrs. Cole's breast cancer had been caught at an early stage, and that her chances for recovery were excellent. The family therapist helped Mr. Cole communicate this to his daughters. He needed to convince Ellie and Sarah that just because their grandmother died of the disease, their mother would not necessarily die as well.

Through open communication, both Ellie and Sarah learned more about cancer. They also learned that their grandmother's cancer had been quite advanced by the time it was discovered, and that her chances for survival had been far worse than their mother's.

The therapist used a family therapy technique known as the Empty Chair, when family members speak to an empty chair that represents an absent family member.

In addition, the therapist used a family therapy technique known as the Empty Chair. During this exercise, family members speak to an empty chair that represents an absent family member. As Mrs. Cole was too ill to go to the first few family therapy sessions, both Ellie and Sarah used the chair to help them express things they really wanted to say to their mother. Ellie claimed that this provided some much-needed relief for her. "I said things that I hadn't been able to say to my mother, like saying that I'm afraid she'll die and then I'll be without her forever. I cried, too. It felt good to finally let it out. I was hurting so much inside."

Once Mrs. Cole was well enough to come to family therapy sessions, she saw that her daughters needed her more than ever. The girls viewed the housekeeper as a wall separating them from their mother. Ellie knew that her mother had wanted to hide her illness from them, but her plan had backfired. Being kept in the dark had only made them feel more afraid.

It was agreed that Mrs. Cole would need some time to herself on the days she underwent chemotherapy. However, Ellie was relieved to hear that she would spend the other afternoons with her daughters as they had always done in the past. The housekeeper was to stay on until Mrs. Cole felt stronger, but she would spend more time doing housework and be less involved with Ellie and Sarah.

Support Groups

The family therapist also suggested that the girls join a support group for young people whose mothers have breast cancer. Fortunately, there was one at the hospital at which their mother was being treated. Ellie found it helpful to talk to other young people who had been through what they were going through. At first, it was hard for her to talk about her mother's illness, even to her best friends. They tried to be nice, but it was clear that they didn't really understand Ellie's situation. Ellie didn't want anyone's pity; that only made her feel worse. But now she could confide in people experiencing the same thing she was.

The family therapist also taught the Coles another family therapy technique that proved beneficial. They were to begin having what she referred to as Caring Days. Caring Days are days during which family members are asked to show caring for one another. On one Caring Day, the family visited the local botanical garden. Ellie had planned that day for her mother because she knew that her mom loved sitting in the beautiful rose garden there. That Caring Day helped Ellie as well, because it was obvious to her that she had thought of something her mother really enjoyed.

Not Always a Happy Ending

The Cole story had a happy ending, but not every case involving life-threatening or chronic illness does. A family therapist is prepared to handle these situations as well. Often, these families are facing a serious crisis, so the family therapist will try to equip them with the best coping skills possible. In many cases, the following therapy goals will be set:

- The therapist encourages family members to learn as much as they can about their family member's illness. It helps most people to know what to expect.
- Healthy family members who feel guilty about being well while their loved one is sick are encouraged to deal with their feelings. Through therapy, they see that their guilt is baseless. The fact that they are healthy allows them to better care for the ill family member.

- Through family therapy, family members become more aware of the ill person's emotional needs. The sick individual may feel cut off or excluded from the rest of the family, when feeling that he or she is important to other family members may be especially meaningful at this time. Family members also learn not to turn the ill person into an invalid unnecessarily. During the early phases of numerous illnesses, there are still many things the person may be able to do. It is vital not to rob someone of those opportunities while trying to be helpful. It is also crucial for the ill person to feel competent and in control for as long as possible.

When someone in the family becomes ill, family roles often shift. Through family therapy, conflicts over who will become responsible for various duties can be worked through.

If the illness is fatal, the family therapist will help the family get through the grieving process. Family members learn that there is no "correct" way to grieve. People experience a broad range of emotions, including anger, sadness, and anxiety. Losing a loved one can be one of the most stressful events a person will ever experience. Some people have a physical reaction as well, such as a loss of appetite or an inability to sleep. In the therapy sessions, family members can freely express their sorrow and feelings of loss so that healing can begin.

Dealing with Loss

Grieving is a normal, healthy reaction to loss. It is also a necessary process that all people go through. The American Association for Marriage and Family Therapy cites the four basic phases of grieving as follows:

1. *Numbness and shock*—This stage usually begins immediately after people hear the news. It frequently lasts until after the funeral.

2. *Feelings of separation*—During this stage, people realize that their loss is real. They must come to terms with the fact that they will never see their loved one again. Survivors begin to miss the person who has died.

3. *Disorganization*—Throughout this phase, grieving people often have trouble concentrating. They may feel anxious and more easily distracted than usual.

4. *Reorganization*—This is the final stage of grieving. People have come to terms with the loss of their loved one. At this stage, individuals start adjusting to the change in their lives.

There are no hard-and-fast rules to follow when it comes to dealing with the loss of a loved one. People move through these stages at their own pace. For some, the real healing begins sooner than it does for others.

For more than fifty years, family therapy has aided families facing an array of challenges. Through the process, millions of people have enhanced their lives and the lives of those closest to them—the people who make up their families. Families are crucial to our nation and to the future of our society, serving as early training grounds for upcoming generations. Family therapy strengthens weak families and also makes strong families stronger.

Glossary

- **biofamilies:** families in which all the members are biologically related

- **chemotherapy:** a treatment for cancer involving the use of chemicals

- **chronic illness:** an ongoing or drawn-out sickness

- **cohabitation family:** a family in which two adults who are not married or otherwise related live together, sometimes with children of their own

- **cross-generational family:** a family in which adults of different generations within a family live together

emotional triangle: a family situation in which two family members who don't get along draw a third person into their interactions

extended family: relatives beyond the married nuclear family, such as grandparents, cousins, aunts, and uncles

family therapy: a form of therapy that changes or enhances the family as a working system

foster family: a "substitute" family for children whose parents are temporarily unable to care for them

halo effect: remembering someone who died as being perfect or saintly

individual counseling: counseling that centers on an individual's behavior and outlook

invalid: a person who is not able to function well because of an illness

joint custody family: a family in which divorced parents share equally the responsibility of taking care of a child married nuclear family: a family that includes a husband, wife, and children

neutral: not taking a side in a dispute

ritual: a regularly performed rite or act

schizophrenia: a chronic, severe, and disabling brain disease that causes a breakdown in the thinking process

short-term therapy: a form of therapy that lasts for a short time period and centers on achieving specific goals

single-parent families: a family with only one parent

stepfamilies: families that are formed when a divorced or widowed person with children remarries

sub-systems: smaller groups that function within a family unit

support group: a group of people who meet on a regular basis to discuss common problems or life issues

Further Resources

Books

Armitage, Ronda. *Family Violence.* Austin, Texas: Raintree Steck-Vaughn, 1999.

Canfield, Jack, Mark Victor Hanson, and Kimberly Kirberger. *Chicken Soup for the Teenage Soul on Tough Stuff: Stories of Tough Times and Lessons Learned.* Deerfield Beach, Florida: Health Communications, 2001.

Carlson, Richard. *Don't Sweat the Small Stuff for Teens.* New York: Hyperion Press, 2000.

Covey, Sean. *Daily Reflections For Highly Effective Teens.* St. Louis, Missouri: Fireside, 1999.

Covey, Sean. *The 7 Habits of Highly Effective Teens.* New York: Simon & Schuster, 1998.

Gaillard Smook, Rachel. *Stepfamilies: How a New Family Works.* Berkeley Heights, New Jersey: Enslow Publishers, 2001.

Graham, Stedman. *Teens Can Make It Happen: Nine Steps for Success.* St. Louis, Missouri: Fireside, 2000.

Hong, Maria. *Family Abuse: A National Epidemic.* Berkeley Heights, New Jersey: Enslow Publishers, 1997.

Johnston, Andrea. *Girls Speak Out: Finding Your True Self.* New York: Scholastic, 1997.

Koubek, Christine Wickert. *Friends, Cliques, and Peer Pressure: Be True to Yourself.* Berkeley Heights: Enslow Publishers, 2002.

Lound, Karen. *Girl Power in the Family.* Minneapolis, Minn.: Lerner Publications Company, 2000.

Rench, Janice E. *Family Violence: How to Recognize and Survive It.* Minneapolis, Minnesota: Lerner Publications Company, 1992.

Stewart, Gail B. *Child Abuse.* San Diego, California: Gale Group, 2003.

Online Sites and Organizations

American Association for Marriage and Family Therapy
112 South Alfred St.
Alexandria, VA 22314
703-838-9808
www.aamft.org

American Group Psychotherapy Association
25 East 21 Street, 6th floor
New York, NY 10010
877-668-2472
www.groupsinc.org

American Psychological Association
750 First Street, NE
Washington, DC 20002-4242
800-374-2721
www.apa.org

Association for Conflict Resolution
1015 18 Street, NW, Suite 1150
Washington, DC 20036
202-464-9700
www.acresolution.org

National Association of School Psychologists
4340 East West Highway, Suite 402
Bethesda, MD 20814
301-657-0270
www.nasponline.org/index2.html

National Association of Social Workers
750 First Street, NE, Suite 700
Washington, DC 20002-4241
202-408-8600
www.naswdc.org

National Council on Family Relations
3989 Central Avenue, NE #550
Minneapolis, MN 55421
888-781-9331
www.ncfr.com

The American Association of Family & Consumer Sciences
1555 King Street
Alexandria, VA 22314
703-706-4600
www.aafcs.org

Index

About the Author

Award-winning author **Elaine Landau** has written more than two hundred books for young readers. She worked as a newspaper reporter, a children's book editor, and a youth services librarian before becoming a full-time writer. Many of her books deal with contemporary issues relevant to young adults. Ms. Landau lives in Miami, Florida, with her husband and son.